AF322706

Flavors of the World

Flavors of the World
World

A Culinary Journey

B. Vincent

QuantumQuill Press

Contents

Chapter 1: Introduction to Global Cuisine

Investigating Culinary Variety:

Set out on a tempting excursion through the kaleidoscope of worldwide flavors as we dive into the rich embroidery of culinary practices from around the world. In this section, we welcome you to relish the assorted fragrances, tastes, and surfaces that portray foods traversing mainlands and societies.

From the fragrant flavors of India to the good stews of Ireland, each edge of the globe offers an exceptional gastronomic encounter formed by hundreds of years of custom and development. Whether it's the umami-rich dishes of Japan or the searing intensity of Mexican food, there's a universe of culinary joys ready to be found.

Go along with us as we commend the unfathomable imagination of culinary experts and home cooks the same, who draw motivation from their social legacy to make dishes that tempt the taste buds and support the spirit. From road food slows down to Michelin-featured cafés, the variety of worldwide cooking is a demonstration of the vast conceivable outcomes of culinary articulation.

Thus, let your taste buds be your aide as we set out on this luxurious experience, investigating the kinds of the world each chomp in turn. Prepare to grow your sense of taste, widen your culinary skylines, and find the genuine substance of worldwide gastronomy. Bon appétit!

Social and Geological Impacts:

Inside the stewing pots and sizzling container of worldwide food lies a rich embroidery of social and geological impacts that shape the manner in which we eat and cook. In this section, we strip back the layers to reveal the significant effect of geology and culture on culinary practices all over the planet.

From the sun-soaked shores of the Mediterranean to the rich rainforests of Southeast Asia, the actual land frequently directs the fixings accessible and the cooking strategies utilized. Whether it's the fish rich eating regimens of beach front networks or the good toll of sloping locales, topographical variables assume a significant part in forming provincial foods.

Similarly huge are the social impacts that instill each dish with importance and custom. From age-old ceremonies to familial recipes went down through ages, food fills in as a strong articulation of personality and legacy. Whether it's the mutual galas of African towns or the intricate tea services of Japan, social works on encompassing food are basically as different as the cooking styles themselves.

As we venture through the culinary scene, we'll investigate how elements like history, relocation, and exchange have additionally improved and broadened worldwide cooking. From the zest shipping lanes of the old world to the cutting edge blend of worker networks, social trade has consistently implanted new flavors and fixings into culinary customs.

In this way, go along with us as we reveal the mind boggling snare of social and geological impacts that unite on our plates, changing simple fixings into culinary show-stoppers that recount the account of mankind's common culinary legacy.

Verifiable Development:

Leave on a journey through time as we follow the entrancing development of worldwide cooking, from its modest starting points to the energetic embroidery of flavors we know today. In this part, we dive into the archives of history to reveal the multifaceted underlying foundations of culinary customs that have been molded by hundreds of years of social trade, triumph, and development.

From the old zest courses that associated the East and West to the provincial journeys that carried new fixings to far off shores, the historical backdrop of food is entwined with the more extensive flows of human progress. We'll investigate how antiquated civic establishments like the Egyptians, Greeks, and Romans laid the foundation for current culinary strategies and fixings, from the development of wheat to the specialty of maturation.

As domains rose and fell, culinary customs kept on developing, mixing flavors and strategies from different societies and areas. We'll dive into the culinary traditions of civilizations, for example, the Silk Street dealers, whose zest loaded bands carried outlandish flavors to the tables of Europe, and the Islamic Brilliant Age, which saw the refinement of culinary expressions and the improvement of complex court cooking styles.

The Time of Investigation opened up new skylines for culinary advancement, as European voyagers navigated the globe looking for flavors, spices, and outlandish fixings. We'll inspect the effect of this worldwide trade on culinary practices, from the acquaintance of bean stew peppers with India by Portuguese dealers to the spread of potatoes and tomatoes from the New World to Europe.

Through wars, movements, and social trades, culinary practices have kept on advancing, adjusting to changing preferences and conditions while holding their fundamental person. Today, as we stand on the shoulders of our culinary predecessors, we praise the rich woven artwork of flavors that demonstrate the veracity of the flexibility, innovativeness, and resourcefulness of humanity.

Key Fixings and Procedures:

Open the mysteries of worldwide food as we investigate the fundamental fixings and methods that structure the groundwork of culinary practices all over the planet. In this part, we'll set out on a culinary odyssey through clamoring markets, sweet-smelling zest slows down, and clamoring kitchens to find the structure blocks of flavor that characterize each culture's extraordinary culinary personality.

From the fragrant flavors of the Center East to the umami-rich sauces of East Asia, each district brags a mark weapons store fixings that loan profundity and intricacy to their dishes. We'll dig into the storeroom staples that structure the foundation of world-wide cooking, from grains like rice and wheat to season enhancers like spices, flavors, and aromatics.

Yet, it's not just about the fixings — it's additionally about the procedures used to change them into delicious dinners. From slow stewing and braising to speedy sautéing and barbecuing, each culinary practice has own collection of cooking techniques feature the normal flavors and surfaces of the fixings. We'll investigate the specialty of sushi-production in Japan, the sensitive cake work of French food, and the searing wok abilities of Chinese pan-searing.

En route, we'll uncover the culinary speculative chemistry behind notable dishes like pasta carbonara, biryani, and ceviche, as well as the social meaning of these dearest works of art. Whether it's becoming amazing at moving sushi or consummating the strategy for creating handcrafted tortillas, we'll give tips and deceives to assist you with lifting your cooking higher than ever.

In this way, focus in and hone your blades as we set out on a culinary experience that will entice your taste buds, light your creative mind, and move you to bring the kinds of the world into your own kitchen.

Embracing Social Appreciation:

Step into the universe of worldwide cooking with an open heart and an inquisitive psyche as we commend the excellence of social variety and the all inclusive language of food. In this part, we'll investigate the significance of social appreciation in culinary investigation, encouraging grasping, regard, and association across lines and limits.

Food has long filled in as a strong extension between societies, rising above language obstructions and cultivating associations between individuals from varying backgrounds. Whether it's imparting a feast to loved ones or investigating the culinary practices of a far off land, food has the exceptional capacity to unite us and praise our common mankind.

As we venture through the culinary scene, we'll figure out how to move toward each dish with a feeling of interest and regard, respecting the social legacy and customs from which it springs. We'll investigate the tales behind the recipes — the customs, fantasies, and legends that pervade each dish with importance and importance — and find the significant associations among food and character.

Be that as it may, social appreciation goes past partaking in the kinds of a specific cooking. It likewise includes figuring out the authentic, social, and political setting in which it created, recognizing the commitments of different networks to the culinary embroidered artwork of mankind. From the customary food varieties of native people groups to the combination cooking styles conceived out of diaspora and relocation, each dish recounts an account of flexibility, variation, and endurance.

Thus, as you set out on your culinary excursion, make sure to enjoy the flavors on your plate, yet additionally the rich woven artwork of culture and custom that encompasses them. By embracing social appreciation in our investigation of worldwide cooking, we can cultivate more noteworthy figuring out, compassion, and association with our general surroundings. Bon appétit!

{ 2 }

Chapter 2: Asian Delights

Kinds of Asia:

Set up your sense of taste for a tempting excursion through the enrapturing foods of Asia, where each dish recounts an account of custom, development, and social legacy. In this section, we welcome you to investigate the assorted flavors that beauty the tables from the clamoring roads of Bangkok to the quiet tea places of Kyoto.

Asia's culinary scene is pretty much as immense and fluctuated as the actual landmass, offering a kaleidoscope of tastes, surfaces, and fragrances to please the faculties. From the red hot intensity of Thai curries to the sensitive equilibrium of flavors in Japanese sushi, every cooking flaunts its own special personality, formed by hundreds of years of custom and creativity.

As we set out on this culinary odyssey, we'll travel through the zest loaded markets of India, where fragrant spices and flavors imbue each dish with an ensemble of flavors. We'll enjoy the umami-rich pleasures of Chinese cooking, with its delicious pansears and heavenly dumplings. What's more, we'll wonder about the flawless creativity of Japanese cooking, where accuracy and effortlessness rule.

In any case, Asian food is something other than a gala for the faculties — it's an impression of the rich embroidery of societies, customs, and chronicles that characterize the locale. From the road food slows down of Vietnam to the imperial kitchens of Thailand, each dish conveys with it an account of strength, variation, and innovativeness.

Thus, go along with us as we set out on this culinary experience through the kinds of Asia, where each nibble is an excursion regardless of anyone else's opinion, and each dinner is a potential chance to praise the energetic variety of our reality. Bon appétit!

Staple Fixings:

As we dig further into the culinary fortunes of Asia, it becomes obvious that the underpinning of its different cooking styles lies in a small bunch of staple fixings that have endured over the extreme long haul. In this segment, we'll unwind the culinary speculative chemistry behind these fundamental components, investigating their social importance, verifiable roots, and adaptable applications across Asian cooking.

Rice, loved as the "staff of life" in numerous Asian societies, becomes the dominant focal point as perhaps of the most key staple. From soft jasmine rice in Thailand to tacky sushi rice in Japan, the horde assortments of rice act as the foundation of endless Asian dishes, giving food and fulfillment in equivalent measure.

Noodles, one more dearest staple, arrive in a bewildering exhibit of shapes, sizes, and surfaces, each loaning its own personality to dishes across the landmass. Whether it's the chewy hand-pulled noodles of China, the gulp commendable ramen of Japan, or the fragrant laksa noodles of Malaysia, noodles play a featuring job in Asian food, offering solace and sustenance to millions.

Flavors and spices, with their inebriating smells and dynamic tones, add profundity and intricacy to Asian dishes, hoisting them from simple food to culinary works of art. From the searing intensity of stew peppers to the fragrant notes of lemongrass and cilantro, these sweet-smelling fixings imbue each dish with an orchestra of flavors that dance on the sense of taste.

However, maybe the most exceptional part of Asian food is its capacity to change humble fixings into culinary miracles through the wizardry of aging and conservation. Soy sauce, miso, and matured bean glues add profundity and extravagance to dishes, while cured vegetables and safeguarded meats offer an eruption of tart newness that slices through rich flavors.

In this way, as we give proper respect to these fundamental fixings that structure the foundation of Asian cooking, let us commend the resourcefulness, imagination, and cleverness of the endless ages who have developed and valued them. For in the modest grains of rice, the strands of noodles, and the fragrant flavors of Asia, we track down food, yet a significant association with the rich embroidery of culinary legacy that ties all of us.

Territorial Varieties:

As we venture across the tremendous territory of Asia, we experience a rich embroidery of local varieties that add profundity and subtlety to the mainland's culinary scene. In this part, we'll investigate the different flavors and cooking styles that rise out of the one of a kind geology, environment, and social legacy of every locale, offering a tempting look into the rich variety of Asian food.

From the sweet-smelling curries of South Asia to the fragile kinds of Southeast Asia, every area flaunts own unmistakable culinary practices mirror its set of experiences, customs, and neighborhood fixings. In India, for instance, the searing intensity of a Punjabi curry stands out from the unpretentious flavors of a Bengali fish dish, exhibiting the mind blowing variety of flavors tracked down inside a solitary country.

Likewise, in Southeast Asia, the lavish tropical scene leads to lively and fragrant dishes that burst with new flavors and strong differences. From the tart pleasantness of Vietnamese pho to the red hot force of Thai tom yum soup, each dish mirrors the wealth of neighborhood fixings and the rich social legacy of the locale.

In any case, it's not just about the fixings — territorial varieties in cooking strategies and planning techniques likewise assume a critical part in forming the kinds of Asian food. In China, for instance, the specialty of sautéing and steaming permits fixings to hold their normal flavors and surfaces, while in Japan, the exact blade work and fragile show of sushi feature the nation's adoration for effortlessness and class.

As we dive further into the culinary practices of Asia, we'll find the rich woven artwork of local fortes that make every cooking remarkable. From the zesty curries of Thailand to the sensitive sushi of Japan, each dish recounts an account of custom, development, and social pride, offering a tempting look into the rich variety of Asian cooking.

Signature Dishes:

Plan to entice your taste buds as we dig into the famous dishes that have come to characterize the culinary scene of Asia. In this segment, we'll set out on a culinary excursion through the landmass, investigating the rich history, social importance, and unmatched kinds of a portion of Asia's most darling manifestations.

First on our culinary visit is Japan, home to sushi, tempura, and ramen — dishes that have spellbound the world with their flawless flavors and careful craftsmanship. From the accuracy of sushi-production to the spirit warming solace of a steaming bowl of ramen, Japanese food exemplifies an ideal harmony between straightforwardness and refinement.

Then, we dare to Thailand, where the strong flavors and energetic shades of dishes like cushion thai, green curry, and mango tacky rice tempt the faculties and transport burger joints to the clamoring roads of Bangkok. With its agreeable mix of sweet, harsh, pungent, and fiery flavors, Thai cooking is a festival of equilibrium and intricacy.

In China, a culinary practice traversing millennia, we experience a confounding exhibit of local strengths, from the red hot intensity of Sichuanese hotpot to the fragile kinds of Cantonese faint total. Each dish recounts an account of the country's different scenes, rich social legacy, and extremely old culinary customs.

As we venture through Asia, we'll likewise find the striking and complex kinds of Indian food, with its fragrant flavors, rich curries, and liberal desserts. From the blazing force of a vindaloo to the smooth solace of a margarine chicken, Indian cooking offers a tangible gala that joys and charms in equivalent measure.

In any case, maybe generally striking of everything is the manner by which these mark dishes rise above lines and limits, filling in as representatives of culture and food to the world. Whether it's partaking in a bowl of pho in Vietnam or relishing a plate of cushion see ew in Thailand, each nibble is a festival of the rich embroidery of flavors that make Asian cooking genuinely remarkable.

Combination Cooking:

In the consistently developing universe of culinary expressions, combination cooking remains as a demonstration of the endless imagination and development of gourmet experts who try to push the limits of custom. In this segment, we'll investigate the thrilling convergence of conventional Asian flavors with present day culinary procedures, bringing about an enticing combination of taste impressions that enamor the sense of taste and touch off the creative mind.

From the roads of Seoul to the high rises of Singapore, combination cooking has overwhelmed Asia, offering an enticing mix of flavors and impacts that mirror the locale's different social scene. In urban communities like Tokyo and Hong Kong, gourmet specialists draw motivation from a bunch of culinary practices, consistently coordinating fixings and strategies from around the world to make dishes that oppose classification.

One of the signs of combination food is its capacity to rise above social limits, uniting fixings and flavors from different culinary customs to make something completely intriguing. In dishes like Korean tacos, sushi burritos, and ramen burgers, conventional Asian fixings are reconsidered and rehashed in unforeseen and delightful ways.

In any case, combination food isn't just about getting flavors from various societies — it's likewise about regarding and regarding those practices while putting an exceptional twist on exemplary dishes. Whether it's adding a hint of sriracha to a customary French sauce or integrating Japanese miso into a Mexican marinade, combination culinary experts approach their art with a feeling of inventiveness, interest, and regard.

As we dig further into the universe of combination food, we'll find the extraordinary variety of flavors and impacts that meet up to make dishes that are all around as interesting and dynamic as the way of life from which they draw motivation. From upscale eateries to road food slows down, combination cooking keeps on pushing the limits of what's conceivable, welcoming burger joints on a culinary experience that rises above lines and shows.

Chapter 3: European Gastronomy

Culinary Legacy of Europe:

Welcome to the support of culinary greatness, where extremely old practices, various scenes, and rich social legacy unite to make an embroidery of flavors that spellbind the faculties and move the spirit. In this segment, we leave on a gastronomic excursion through the core of Europe, investigating the culinary legacy that has molded the mainland's different foods.

Europe's culinary scene is essentially as changed and multi-layered as its topography, with every locale flaunting its own novel fixings, cooking methods, and flavor profiles. From the provincial effortlessness of Mediterranean food to the generous passage of Focal Europe, the mainland offers a tempting exhibit of culinary pleasures ready to be found.

At the core of European gastronomy lies a profound worship for custom and quality, with many dishes and strategies went down through ages. Whether it's the specialty of cheddar making in the French open country or the revered custom of charcuterie in Italy,

European food is saturated with history and craftsmanship, with each dish recounting an account of social personality and pride.

In any case, it's not just about the food — it's additionally about the experience. In Europe, eating is an esteemed custom, a chance to assemble with loved ones, relishing the basic delights of good food and great organization. From energetic road markets to Michelin-featured eateries, the mainland offers an abundance of culinary encounters to suit each sense of taste and spending plan.

As we venture through the culinary legacy of Europe, we'll dig into the rich embroidery of flavors, fixings, and customs that characterize every area's special culinary personality. From the grape plantations of France to the olive forests of Italy, each nibble is a festival of the immortal upsides of craftsmanship, quality, and cordiality that have made European cooking a signal of greatness for a really long time. Bon appétit!

Ranch to-Table Way of thinking:

In the verdant fields and prolific valleys of Europe, a culinary unrest is in progress — a re-visitation of the underlying foundations of gastronomy, where the excursion from ranch to table is praised and worshipped. In this segment, we dive into the homestead to-table way of thinking that has reshaped European gastronomy, supporting the temperances of new, privately obtained fixings and economical farming practices.

At the core of the homestead to-table development lies a profound appreciation for the regular abundance of the land and the significance of safeguarding it for people in the future. Across Europe, culinary experts and customers the same are rediscovering the delights of occasional eating, embracing the flavors and surfaces of fixings reaped at the pinnacle of readiness and flavor.

From the grape plantations of Tuscany to the olive forests of Greece, Europe's horticultural scene is essentially as different as its culinary practices, offering a gold mine of fixings ready to be investigated. Whether it's legacy tomatoes from the south of France or high quality cheeses from the Swiss Alps, the ranch to-table way of thinking commends the rich variety of flavors that must be seen as up close and personal.

In any case, the ranch to-table development is about something other than the food — it's likewise about manufacturing associations between makers, cooks, and customers, encouraging a feeling of local area and shared liability regarding the land and its abundance. By supporting neighborhood ranchers and makers, we not just guarantee the newness and nature of our food yet additionally add to the wellbeing and essentialness of our networks and biological systems.

As we embrace the ranch to-table way of thinking, we honor the ageless upsides of craftsmanship, stewardship, and supportability that have characterized European gastronomy for ages. From the fields and fields to the kitchen table, let us relish the kinds of the land and praise the abundance of nature in each delectable nibble.

French Food:

Enter the domain of culinary greatness and refinement as we investigate the notable cooking of France — an immortal festival of flavor, procedure, and masterfulness that has enthralled palates all over the planet. In this part, we dig into the rich embroidery of French culinary practices, from the clamoring markets of Provence to the blessed lobbies of haute cooking in Paris.

French food is prestigious for its fastidious meticulousness, its accentuation on quality fixings, and its steadfast obligation to culinary greatness. From the sensitive sauces of Escoffier to the natural effortlessness of laborer dishes, French cooking is a masterclass in equilibrium, concordance, and accuracy, where each dish is a show-stopper regardless of anyone else's opinion.

At the core of French cooking lies a profound respect for custom and terroir, with every district flaunting its own interesting strengths and culinary legacy. From the rich croissants of Brittany to the generous cassoulets of Gascony, the variety of flavors and fixings found across France is a demonstration of the country's rich social embroidery.

In any case, maybe generally momentous of everything is the manner by which French cooking proceeds to advance and develop, embracing new fixings, strategies, and impacts while staying consistent with its immortal standards of craftsmanship and quality. Whether it's the vanguard manifestations of sub-atomic gastronomy or the creative turns on exemplary dishes found in current bistros, French food is as unique and energizing as anyone might imagine.

As we venture through the culinary scene of France, we'll find the enthusiasm, innovativeness, and imaginativeness that have made it a signal of culinary greatness for quite a long time. From the humblest bistro to the most fantastic castle, each feast is a festival of the rich social legacy and gastronomic customs that characterize French food. Bon appétit!

Italian Flavors:

Plan to be moved to the sun-soaked slopes of Tuscany and the clamoring piazzas of Rome as we set out on a culinary excursion through the dynamic kinds of Italy. In this segment, we praise the immortal charm of Italian cooking — a festival of straightforwardness, quality fixings, and the delight of get-together around the table with loved ones.

Italian food is darling the world over for its natural appeal, its intense flavors, and its steady obligation to custom. From the brilliant fields of wheat that yield the best pasta to the fragrant forests of olive trees that produce the best olive oil, Italy's normal abundance is reflected in each dish, from the humblest trattoria to the most stupendous Michelin-featured café.

At the core of Italian cooking lies a love for the seasons, with dishes changing with the rhythmic movement of nature's abundance. From the new kinds of springtime asparagus and artichokes to the generous solace of winter's stews and braises, Italian cooking is a festival of the lavishness and variety of the Italian scene.

In any case, maybe generally cherished of all are the famous dishes that have come to characterize Italian food — the spirit warming solace of a steaming bowl of spaghetti carbonara, the velvety debauchery of an impeccably cooked risotto, the fresh flawlessness of a wood-terminated pizza. Each dish recounts an account of custom, legacy, and the immortal upsides of craftsmanship and quality that have made Italian cooking a worldwide peculiarity.

As we appreciate the kinds of Italy, let us commend the basic joys of good food, great wine, and great organization. Whether it's a comfortable Sunday lunch with family or a merry supper with companions, Italian food welcomes us to dial back, enjoy the experience, and revel in the delight of shared feasts and enduring recollections. Buon appetito!

Spanish Tapas and that's only the tip of the iceberg:

Step into the dynamic embroidery of Spanish food, where each dish is a festival of flavor, energy, and the delight of shared dinners. In this part, we investigate the rich culinary legacy of Spain, from the sun-soaked shores of Andalusia to the rough scenes of Catalonia, revealing the assorted flavors and customs that make Spanish food genuinely extraordinary.

At the core of Spanish cooking lies a profound appreciation for the straightforward joys of good food and great organization. No place is this more obvious than in the custom of tapas — a culinary custom that unites loved ones to share little plates of delightful dishes, from firm croquettes to delicious barbecued fish.

However, Spanish cooking is about something other than tapas — it's a festival of the country's rich social legacy and various local flavors. From the strong flavors of Moorish-impacted dishes in the south to the good stews and frankfurters of the north, Spain's culinary scene is all around as shifted and lively as its scenes and customs.

One of the signs of Spanish cooking is its utilization of new, privately obtained fixings, from the best tomatoes to the best olive oil. Whether it's the tart pleasantness of an entirely ready tomato in a gazpacho or the smoky wealth of a chorizo hotdog in a paella, Spanish dishes are a demonstration of the quality and overflow of the country's regular abundance.

As we venture through the kinds of Spain, let us raise a glass to the rich embroidery of flavors and customs that make Spanish cooking a blowout for the faculties. Whether it's a relaxed feast at a clamoring tapas bar or a bubbly social event with loved ones, Spanish cooking welcomes us to embrace the delight of shared dinners and enduring recollections. ¡Buen provecho!

{ 4 }

Chapter 4: Taste of the Americas

Culinary Variety:

Welcome to the blend of flavors and customs that is the Americas, a tremendous and different mainland where culinary inventiveness exceeds all logical limitations. In this part, we set out on an excursion through the rich embroidery of culinary practices that have thrived across North and South America, molded by hundreds of years of social trade and development.

American food is a demonstration of the extraordinary variety of individuals who call this land home, mirroring a dynamic combination of native, European, African, and Asian impacts. From the good stews and corn-based dishes of Local American clans to the complicated zest mixes and cooking strategies brought by European pilgrims, American food is a festival of the bunch flavors and fixings that have met up to make something genuinely special.

At the core of this culinary variety lies a feeling of trial and error and transformation, as various societies and customs cross and impact each other, making intriguing flavor mixes. Whether it's the red hot intensity of Mexican bean stew peppers, the smoky extravagance of Southern grill, or the fragile kinds of Peruvian ceviche, American food is a demonstration of the vast conceivable outcomes of culinary investigation.

In any case, it's not just about the flavors — it's additionally about the narratives behind the dishes, the practices that have been gone down through ages, and the associations that food makes between individuals. Whether it's social event around the table for a vacation blowout or imparting recipes to loved ones, food has an ability to interest to unite us and praise our common mankind.

As we venture through the culinary variety of the Americas, let us relish the flavors, embrace the customs, and commend the rich embroidery of societies that make American food an impression of individuals who call this mainland home. From the clamoring roads of New York City to the distant towns of the Amazon rainforest, each dish recounts a story — an account of flexibility, innovativeness, and the force of food to join all of us. Bon appétit!

Native Fixings:

Enter the domain of old practices and holy flavors as we investigate the rich culinary legacy of native people groups across the Americas. In this part, we give recognition to the respected fixings and cooking procedures that have supported networks for centuries, established in a profound veneration for the land and its abundance.

Native food is a festival of concordance with nature, with fixings obtained straightforwardly from the land, streams, and woods that have supported networks for ages. From the holy maize of the Maya to the good beans and squash of the Haudenosaunee, these conventional staples structure the foundation of native eating regimens, giving food and sustenance in overflow.

However, native food is about something beyond food — it's likewise an impression of culture, otherworldliness, and association with the land. Numerous fixings hold profound social importance, with customs and functions revolved around their development, reap, and readiness. From the sacrosanct customs of corn planting among the Hopi to the formal dining experiences of the Inuit, food fills in as a strong articulation of personality and local area.

Lately, there has been a developing acknowledgment of the significance of native foodways in advancing wellbeing, maintainability, and social flexibility. Endeavors to recover conventional food sources and cooking strategies have ignited a renaissance of native cooking, with gourmet specialists and activists attempting to save and praise the culinary legacy of their precursors.

As we honor the native fixings and customs of the Americas, let us likewise recognize the difficulties and shameful acts looked by native networks, from land dispossession to social eradication. By supporting native drove drives and embracing the extravagance of their culinary legacy, we can add to a more impartial and comprehensive future for all.

Latin American Flavors:

Leave on an excursion through the energetic and various culinary scenes of Latin America, where each dish recounts an account of custom, development, and social pride. In this segment, we investigate the rich woven artwork of flavors that characterize the cooking styles of nations like Mexico, Brazil, Peru, and Argentina, commending the novel fixings, methods, and customs that make every food so exceptional.

Latin American food is a festival of overflow, with dishes overflowing with strong flavors, lively tones, and a tempting exhibit of fixings. From the tart citrus of Peruvian ceviche to the smoky extravagance of Mexican mole, the variety of flavors found across Latin America is a demonstration of the mainland's rich social legacy and culinary practices.

At the core of Latin American food lies a profound love for the land and its abundance, with many dishes drawing motivation from native fixings and cooking strategies. Whether it's the old practice of nixtamalization in Mexico, the specialty of broiling meats over an open fire in Argentina, or the sensitive equilibrium of flavors in Brazilian feijoada, Latin American cooking is saturated with history, culture, and custom.

Yet, Latin American food is likewise an impression of the locale's rich social embroidery, with impacts from Africa, Europe, and Asia adding profundity and intricacy to dishes. From the searing flavors of African-propelled moqueca to the generous stews and meals brought by European pioneers, Latin American cooking is a blend of flavors, strategies, and culinary practices.

As we venture through the kinds of Latin America, let us enjoy the extravagance and variety of the locale's culinary legacy, commending the flexibility, innovativeness, and resourcefulness of individuals who have formed it. From the clamoring markets of Mexico City to the far off towns of the Andes, each dish is a demonstration of the excellence and intricacy of Latin American cooking. ¡Buen provecho!

Southern fare and Southern Solace:

Step into the warm hug of Southern neighborliness as we investigate the rich culinary customs of the American South — a place that is known for profound flavors, good solace food, and a profound feeling of custom. In this segment, we dig into the famous dishes and social meaning of Southern food, praising the flavors and stories that have been gone down through ages.

Southern fare, with its underlying foundations in the African American people group, is a festival of strength, imagination, and creativity notwithstanding misfortune. From the delicate hug of slow-cooked collard greens to the firm flawlessness of broiled chicken, southern fare dishes are a demonstration of the genius of oppressed Africans and their relatives, who changed humble fixings into culinary works of art.

However, Southern cooking is about something beyond southern fare — it's likewise an impression of the district's different social legacy, with impacts from Local American, European, and Caribbean foods adding profundity and intricacy to dishes. Whether it's the Cajun flavors of Louisiana, the Lowcountry kinds of South Carolina, or the Tex-Mex combination of the Southwest, Southern food is a mixture of flavors and customs.

At the core of Southern cooking lies a profound respect for custom and local area, with many dishes filling in as an extension among at various times, interfacing ages through shared dinners and valued recipes. From family gatherings and church picnics to occasion dining experiences and Sunday dinners, food assumes a focal part in Southern culture, uniting individuals and supporting the obligations of family and fellowship.

As we relish the kinds of the American South, let us likewise recognize the perplexing history and social inheritance that has formed Southern cooking. By regarding the practices and stories behind each dish, we can commend the versatility, inventiveness, and persevering through soul of individuals who have made Southern cooking a darling and getting through piece of American culture. So take a seat, pass the cornbread, and let the kinds of the South vehicle you to a spot where neighborliness rules and each dinner is a festival of life.

Combination and Development:

Enter the domain of culinary imagination and development as we investigate the powerful scene of combination food reshaping the flavor of the Americas. In this part, we witness the thrilling impact of culinary customs, strategies, and flavors, as gourmet experts and food devotees push the limits of custom to make something completely new and startling.

Combination food in the Americas is an impression of the district's different social embroidery, with impacts from around the world meeting up to make dishes that oppose classification. Whether it's the Japanese-propelled sushi burritos of California, the Korean-injected tacos of Los Angeles, or the Peruvian-Japanese combination of Nikkei cooking, combination gourmet experts draw motivation from a horde of culinary practices to make dishes that are however special as they may be heavenly.

Yet, combination cooking is about something other than joining fixings — it's likewise about rethinking customary dishes and procedures in imaginative and unforeseen ways. Whether it's integrating Latin American flavors into exemplary American solace food sources or imbuing Asian fixings with Caribbean flavors, combination culinary specialists approach their art with a feeling of inventiveness, trial and error, and investigation.

At the core of combination cooking lies a feeling of joint effort and multifaceted trade, with culinary specialists and food lovers drawing motivation from a different scope of impacts to make dishes that mirror the lavishness and variety of the Americas. By embracing combination cooking, we commend the associations that join us across boundaries and societies, and perceive the extraordinary force of food to connect partitions and encourage understanding.

As we investigate the universe of combination food in the Americas, let us relish the striking flavors, imaginative strategies, and startling pairings that make it such a lively and energizing culinary scene. From food trucks and spring up eateries to fancy foundations, combination cooking welcomes us to leave on a culinary experience where each chomp is a festival of innovativeness, variety, and the endless potential outcomes of the human sense of taste. Bon appétit!

Chapter 5: African Culinary Heritage

Prologue to African Food:

Step into a universe of lively flavors, rich customs, and exceptionally old culinary legacy as we set out on an excursion through the different and dynamic scene of African cooking. In this segment, we set up for investigation, offering a brief look into the kaleidoscope of tastes, surfaces, and fragrances that characterize the culinary embroidery of the African mainland.

African food is basically as different as the actual mainland, with every district flaunting its own special fixings, cooking procedures, and flavor profiles. From the red hot intensity of North African tagines to the generous stews and cassava-based dishes of West Africa, the broadness and profundity of African food are a demonstration of the landmass' rich social mosaic and complex history.

At the core of African cooking lies a profound veneration for custom and local area, with food filling in as a foundation of get-togethers, festivities, and transitional experiences. From the shared banquets of the Maasai in East Africa to the intricate food customs of the Yoruba in West Africa, African cooking is mixed with imagery, meaning, and a significant feeling of association with the land and its kin.

Yet, African cooking isn't just about the food — it's additionally about the accounts behind the dishes, the ceremonies that encompass them, and the qualities they encapsulate. Whether it's the versatility and cleverness of customary cooking methods went down through ages or the soul of development and imagination driving contemporary translations of African food, each dish recounts an account of social character, strength, and pride.

As we set out on this culinary odyssey through the kinds of Africa, let us enjoy the lavishness and variety of the landmass' culinary legacy, praising the inventiveness, imagination, and flexibility of individuals who have formed it. From the sun-doused savannas of the Serengeti to the clamoring markets of Marrakech, each nibble is an excursion no matter what anyone else might think, welcoming us to investigate, find, and take pleasure in the endless potential outcomes of African food. Karibu!

Customary Fixings and Cooking Methods:

Enter the core of African culinary practices as we dive into the rich woven artwork of conventional fixings and cooking strategies that have supported networks across the mainland for a really long time. In this part, we uncover the mysteries of native African food, commending the abundance of the land and the clever manners by which African cooks change straightforward fixings into culinary magnum opuses.

African cooking is well established in the land, with numerous conventional dishes drawing motivation from privately obtained fixings that are developed, searched, or chased from the general climate. Grains like millet, sorghum, and teff structure the premise of many staple dishes, giving food and sustenance to millions across the mainland. Tubers like sweet potatoes, cassava, and yams are likewise indispensable to African cooking, offering a generous and fulfilling starting point for stews, soups, and porridges.

In any case, it's not just about the fixings — likewise about the cooking strategies have been consummated over ages, went down through oral custom and sharpened through hundreds of years of training. From the sluggish stewing of stews and soups over an open fire to the many-sided zest mixes and marinades used to enhance meats and vegetables, African cooking is a demonstration of the inventiveness, cleverness, and innovativeness of its kin.

One of the signs of African food is its accentuation on public feasting, with dinners frequently served family-style and divided between friends and family. Whether it's the intricate galas of extraordinary events like weddings and celebrations or the straightforward, regular feasts delighted in with loved ones, food fills in as a strong articulation of neighborliness, liberality, and local area.

As we investigate the customary fixings and cooking strategies of African food, let us additionally recognize the social variety and intricacy of the landmass' culinary scene. From the lavish rainforests of Focal Africa to the parched deserts of the Sahara, every locale flaunts its own one of a kind flavors, fixings, and cooking customs, offering an enticing look into the rich embroidery of African culinary legacy. Karibu sana!

Provincial Varieties:

Leave on a culinary undertaking across the different and charming districts of Africa, where every region flaunts its own particular flavors, fixings, and culinary traditions. In this segment, we cross the mainland, investigating the rich embroidered artwork of provincial varieties that loan profundity and intricacy to African cooking.

From the sun-soaked shores of North Africa to the lavish rainforests of Focal Africa, every locale's culinary character is formed by its interesting geology, environment, and social legacy. In North Africa, for instance, the impact of Middle Easterner, Berber, and Mediterranean cooking styles is obvious in the fragrant tagines, couscous dishes, and mezze spreads that beauty tables across the area. In the mean time, in West Africa, the lively kinds of hot jollof rice, generous fufu, and delicious barbecued meats mirror the locale's different social impacts and rich culinary customs.

In East Africa, the abundance of the land and ocean gives a cornucopia of fixings to dishes like Ethiopian injera, Kenyan nyama choma, and Tanzanian pilau. Here, flavors like cardamom, cloves, and cinnamon implant dishes with warmth and intricacy, while new spices and vegetables add splendor and profundity to each nibble.

Moving toward the south, the culinary scene of Southern Africa is molded by a mix of native fixings and European impacts, bringing about dishes like South African bobotie, Mozambican peri chicken, and Namibian kapana. Here, intense flavors and good dishes mirror the area's rich social embroidered artwork and profound association with the land.

In any case, paying little mind to locale, one thing stays steady: the significance of food for of festivity, local area, and social articulation. Whether it's the intricate blowouts of unique events like weddings and celebrations or the basic, regular feasts delighted in with loved ones, African food fills in as a strong sign of the bonds that join us and the extravagance of our common legacy.

As we venture through the local varieties of African food, let us appreciate the variety and intricacy of flavors that make every district special, praising the culinary practices and social fortunes that have thrived across the mainland for a really long time. Karibu!

Social Importance:

Jump into the rich embroidered artwork of African culture as we investigate the significant meaning of food in molding customs, ceremonies, and local area associations across the mainland. In this part, we reveal the well established social implications implanted inside African cooking, enlightening the manners by which food fills in as a strong articulation of character, legacy, and having a place.

In numerous African societies, food isn't just food — it is a sacrosanct gift from the land, an image of overflow and flourishing, and a method for cultivating social bonds and solidarity. From the mutual blowouts of unique events like weddings, births, and collect celebrations to the close social occasions of loved ones, food assumes a focal part in uniting individuals, reinforcing connections, and encouraging a feeling of having a place.

Yet, food in African culture is additionally pervaded with profound importance, with many dishes and fixings conveying emblematic implications and associations with hereditary practices. Whether it's the custom butcher of a creature to stamp an extraordinary event or the readiness of conventional dishes went down through ages, food fills in as a conductor for respecting the past, interfacing with the present, and imagining what's in store.

Notwithstanding its part in friendly and profound life, African food is likewise a strong type of social articulation, with each dish recounting an account of history, movement, and social trade. From the hot kinds of North African tagines to the searing intensity of West African jollof rice, African cooking mirrors the variety and intricacy of the mainland's social legacy, offering a tempting look into the lives and customs of its kin.

As we commend the social meaning of African food, let us additionally recognize the versatility, innovativeness, and resourcefulness of individuals who have protected and enhanced these culinary customs for ages. By embracing African cooking, we honor the extravagance and variety of the landmass' social legacy, and perceive the force of food to join us, motivate us, and sustain both body and soul. Karibu sana!

Contemporary Patterns and Future Standpoint:

Enter the intriguing universe of current African cooking, where custom meets advancement and innovativeness has no limits. In this segment, we investigate the advancing scene of African culinary practices, praising the manners by which gourmet specialists, home cooks, and food lovers are rethinking conventional dishes and procedures to make something altogether new and surprising.

Lately, there has been a resurgence of interest in African cooking both on the mainland and all over the planet, driven by a developing appreciation for its strong flavors, energetic fixings, and rich social legacy. Culinary experts and restaurateurs are drawing motivation from conventional dishes and fixings to make imaginative combination cooking that gives proper respect to the past while embracing what's in store.

From upscale fancy foundations to clamoring road food markets, African cooking is encountering a renaissance, with culinary experts and business people pushing the limits of custom to make dishes that are however outwardly shocking as they seem to be tasty. Whether it's the cutting edge understandings of Nigerian suya presented with a wind, the reexamination of South African rabbit chow with connoisseur pizazz, or the combination of African and Asian flavors in dishes like Mozambican-Thai fish curry, contemporary African food is a festival of imagination, variety, and culinary greatness.

However, the fate of African cooking reaches out past the kitchen — it's additionally about engaging networks, advancing manageability, and saving social legacy. Drives like ranch to-table feasting, culinary the travel industry, and food training programs are assisting with supporting neighborhood ranchers and makers, advance reasonable rural practices, and safeguard conventional culinary information for people in the future.

As we plan ahead for African cooking, let us praise the flexibility, imagination, and resourcefulness of individuals who have molded it, and embrace the rich embroidery of flavors, customs, and stories that make African food an energetic and fundamental piece of the worldwide culinary scene. From the clamoring markets of Lagos to the in vogue diners of Cape Town, the fate of African cooking is brilliant, striking, and loaded with plausibility. Karibu kwa mapishi ya kisasa!

Chapter 6: Exploring Global Fusion

Combination Cooking Characterized:

Welcome to the universe of combination cooking, where culinary limits obscure, and inventiveness knows no restrictions. In this part, we leave on an excursion to unwind the quintessence of combination cooking, diving into its definition, importance, and the imaginativeness behind its creation.

Combination food is a culinary peculiarity that rises above conventional limits, flawlessly mixing components from different culinary customs to make dishes that are however innovative as they may be tasty. At its center, combination cooking addresses a blend of flavors, procedures, and fixings, where culinary development blossoms with the crossing point of societies and foods.

The magnificence of combination cooking lies in its capacity to rise above social and geological boundaries, drawing motivation from remote of the globe to make dishes that challenge arrangement. Whether it's the marriage of Japanese sushi with Mexican flavors in sushi burritos or the combination of Indian flavors with English fixings in chicken tikka masala, combination food praises the variety of the human sense of taste and the vast conceivable outcomes of culinary imagination.

In any case, combination cooking is something other than a culinary pattern — it's an impression of the interconnectedness of our reality, where social trade and globalization have united individuals and thoughts more than ever. In a period of expanding variety and social trade, combination cooking fills in as a strong image of solidarity, resistance, and understanding, advising us that our disparities make us genuinely extraordinary.

As we dive into the universe of combination food, let us embrace the soul of trial and error, interest, and joint effort that characterizes this culinary wilderness. Whether you're a carefully prepared gourmet expert or a brave home cook, combination food welcomes you to push the limits of custom, investigate new flavors and procedures, and commend the rich embroidery of culinary variety that makes our reality so scrumptiously different. Bon appétit!

Social Impacts:

Investigate the mind boggling embroidered artwork of social impacts that shape the energetic scene of combination food, where extremely old customs impact and mix to make culinary magnum opuses. In this segment, we leave on an excursion through history, following the underlying foundations of combination food to the junction of relocation, colonization, and globalization.

Combination cooking is an impression of the rich embroidery of human experience, drawing motivation from the different societies and culinary customs that have molded our reality. From the zest shipping lanes of antiquated times to the floods of movement that have cleared across mainlands, combination cooking is saturated with the historical backdrop of social trade and communication.

One of the vital drivers of combination food is imperialism, which united individuals from various regions of the planet, each bringing their own culinary practices and fixings. The outcome was a combination of flavors and methods that led to previously unheard-of dishes, for example, the Indo-Caribbean curries of Trinidad and Tobago or the Creole cooking styles of the Americas.

Globalization has additionally sped up the spread of combination cooking, as gourmet specialists and food aficionados all over the planet embrace the variety of flavors and fixings accessible to them. Today, combination food mirrors the interconnectedness of our reality, with dishes that draw motivation from societies as different as Japanese, Mexican, Indian, and Italian.

Yet, maybe in particular, combination food fills in as a festival of social variety and the magnificence of social trade. By embracing the flavors and customs of various societies, combination food cultivates figuring out, resistance, and appreciation for the rich embroidered artwork of human experience.

As we investigate the social impacts behind combination food, let us praise the associations that join us and the variety that makes our reality so delightfully perplexing. Whether you're testing sushi tacos in California or kimchi quesadillas in Seoul, combination cooking welcomes you to set out on a culinary excursion that rises above borders and commends the magnificence of social trade. Bon journey!

Notable Combination Dishes:

Get ready to entice your taste buds with a grandstand of notable combination dishes that have enamored food sweethearts all over the planet. In this part, we leave on a culinary experience, investigating the creative and unforeseen mixes of flavors, fixings, and strategies that characterize the universe of combination food.

Notable combination dishes are the embodiment of culinary imagination, mixing components from various culinary practices to make something altogether especially intriguing. From the Japanese-roused sushi burritos of California to the Korean-implanted tacos of Los Angeles, combination cooking delights the sense of taste with its intense flavors, creative introductions, and perky turns on natural top choices.

One such model is the curry pizza, a delectable mashup of Indian flavors and Italian pizza mixture that has turned into a staple in many regions of the planet. The marriage of rich curry sauce, delicate chicken, and sweet-smelling flavors on a fresh pizza hull is a demonstration of the sorcery of combination cooking, where apparently different fixings meet up to make concordance on the plate.

Another notorious combination dish is the banh mi burger, which takes motivation from the exemplary Vietnamese banh mi sandwich and changes it into a delicious burger overflowing with flavor. With its blend of exquisite barbecued meats, cured vegetables, and rich aioli, the banh mi burger offers a brilliant combination of East and West that fulfills the hankering for both solace food and colorful flavors.

However, maybe the most notorious combination dish of everything is the sushi burrito, an amazing creation that consolidates the flavors and surfaces of sushi with the comfort of a handheld wrap. With its brilliant cluster of new fish, fresh vegetables, and flavorful sauces enclosed by a layer of rice and ocean growth, the sushi burrito is a culinary wonder that exemplifies the soul of combination cooking in each nibble.

As we investigate these notable combination dishes, let us commend the inventiveness, innovativeness, and creative mind of the cooks and food devotees who have embraced combination cooking for the purpose of pushing the limits of custom and investigating new culinary boondocks. Whether you're enjoying a fiery fish roll taco or a Korean bar-b-que pizza, combination cooking welcomes you to leave on a gastronomic excursion that knows no restrictions. Bon appétit!

Combination Methods and Patterns:

Dive into the masterfulness of combination food as we investigate the methods and patterns driving development in the culinary world. In this segment, we unwind the mysteries behind making amicable and energizing combination dishes, from fixing replacement to social reevaluation, and look at the most recent patterns molding the eventual fate of combination food.

At the core of combination food lies a feeling of trial and error and imagination, with gourmet experts and home cooks the same embracing a great many methods to mix flavors, surfaces, and culinary practices. Fixing replacement is one such method, where natural fixings are traded out for unforeseen choices to make previously unheard-of flavor blends. Whether it's utilizing Korean gochujang instead of conventional grill sauce or subbing plant-based elements for meat and dairy, fixing replacement permits culinary specialists to push the limits of flavor and reconsider exemplary dishes in new and startling ways.

One more key method in combination cooking is flavor matching, where apparently dissimilar fixings are joined to make surprising concordance on the sense of taste. From the sweet and exquisite mix of pineapple and bacon to the striking differentiation of hot stew and cooling mint, flavor matching permits gourmet specialists to make dishes that are both astounding and fulfilling.

Social reevaluation is likewise a typical procedure in combination cooking, where customary dishes and fixings are rethought from the perspective of various culinary practices. Whether it's putting a cutting edge curve on an exemplary dish or mixing components from various societies to make something completely new, social reevaluation permits gourmet experts to commend the variety of culinary customs while making dishes that are particularly their own.

Lately, a few patterns have arisen in the realm of combination food, reflecting more extensive changes in taste inclinations, dietary inclinations, and culinary development. Plant-based combination, for instance, has acquired ubiquity as additional individuals embrace veggie lover and vegetarian slims down, prompting the making of inventive dishes that feature the flexibility and kind of plant-based fixings. Local combination is another pattern, where gourmet specialists draw motivation from explicit areas or foods to make dishes that praise the variety of worldwide culinary customs.

As we investigate the strategies and patterns molding the eventual fate of combination cooking, let us commend the imagination, variety, and resourcefulness of the gourmet specialists and food lovers who keep on pushing the limits of culinary development. Whether you're trying different things with new flavor mixes in your own kitchen or examining the most recent combination manifestations at an in vogue café, combination cooking welcomes you to embrace receptiveness, interest, and imagination in your culinary undertakings. Bon appétit!

Embracing Variety and Imagination:

Enter an existence where culinary limits disintegrate, and creative mind rules as we commend the variety and imagination intrinsic in combination cooking. In this last area, we ponder the groundbreaking force of food to connect societies, move development, and cultivate association, welcoming you to embrace receptiveness, interest, and joint effort in your culinary excursion.

Combination food is a festival of social trade, where flavors and procedures from around the world meet up to make dishes that rise above conventional limits. Whether it's the combination of Asian, Latin American, and European impacts in a solitary dish or the energetic reevaluation of exemplary top picks through a multicultural focal point, combination cooking welcomes us to investigate new flavors, extend our culinary skylines, and praise the excellence of variety.

At its center, combination food is an impression of the human experience, where shared feasts and shared customs act as a strong wake up call of our normal mankind. By embracing the flavors and elements of various societies, combination food encourages figuring out, sympathy, and appreciation for the lavishness and intricacy of our reality.

However, combination food is likewise a festival of inventiveness, welcoming gourmet experts and home cooks the same to try, develop, and push the limits of custom. Whether you're investigating new flavor mixes, reconsidering exemplary dishes, or teaming up with others to make something completely new, combination cooking urges us to embrace the soul of interest, creative mind, and revelation in our culinary undertakings.

As we commend the variety and imagination of combination food, let us additionally perceive the significance of social responsiveness, regard, and appreciation in our culinary investigations. By regarding the customs and elements of various societies, we can make dishes that charm the sense of taste as well as encourage grasping, association, and common regard.

Thus, whether you're enjoying a sushi burrito, testing kimchi quesadillas, or exploring different avenues regarding your own combination manifestations in the kitchen, let combination food be a sign of the excellence and wealth of our common culinary legacy.

Bon appétit, and may your culinary undertakings be pretty much as different and invigorating as the kinds of combination food!

Chapter 7: The Future of Food

Economical Agribusiness and Cultivating:

Step into an existence where the eventual fate of food is grounded in supportability, as we investigate creative rural practices and cultivating methods pointed toward sustaining the two individuals and the planet. In this part, we dig into the extraordinary force of supportable agribusiness, from vertical cultivating to regenerative practices, and look at its basic job in tending to the squeezing difficulties of food security, natural corruption, and environmental change.

Maintainable farming is something other than a popular expression — it's a promise to developing food such that jelly and renews normal assets, limits natural effect, and guarantees the drawn out reasonability of our food frameworks. One such work on getting some forward momentum is upward cultivating, where harvests are filled in upward stacked layers under controlled conditions, utilizing fundamentally less water and land than conventional cultivating strategies. By expanding space and limiting information sources, vertical cultivating offers a promising answer for the developing interest for new, privately obtained produce in metropolitan regions, while decreasing the carbon impression related with transportation and dissemination.

Regenerative horticulture is one more key part of supportable cultivating, zeroing in on building sound soils, reestablishing biodiversity, and sequestering carbon through comprehensive land the executives rehearses. By consolidating procedures, for example, cover trimming, rotational touching, and agroforestry, regenerative ranchers are further developing soil wellbeing and richness as well as relieving the impacts of environmental change by catching carbon in the dirt and diminishing ozone harming substance emanations.

In any case, practical horticulture is about something other than how we develop our food — it's additionally about who approaches it and how it's disseminated. By supporting limited scope ranchers, putting resources into nearby food frameworks, and elevating evenhanded admittance to nutritious food, we can assemble stronger and comprehensive food frameworks that focus on the prosperity of individuals and the planet.

As we investigate the eventual fate of maintainable horticulture and cultivating, let us additionally perceive the earnestness of making a move to address the interconnected difficulties of food security, natural supportability, and social value. By embracing creative arrangements and cooperating to construct a more supportable food framework, we can guarantee a more brilliant and more fed future for a long time into the future.

Innovation and Food Advancement:

Enter the domain of food development, where innovation fills in as an impetus for extraordinary change by they way we produce, disseminate, and devour food. In this part, we dive into the state of the art headways molding the eventual fate of food, from lab-developed meat and plant-based options in contrast to the digitization of food conveyance and the coordination of brilliant kitchen machines.

Innovation is upsetting each part of the food business, offering answers for probably the most squeezing difficulties we face, from taking care of a developing worldwide populace to lessening the natural effect of food creation. One of the most thrilling improvements is the rise of lab-developed meat and plant-based other options, which offer a maintainable and moral option in contrast to customary creature farming. By refined meat cells in a lab setting or outfitting plant-based proteins to copy the taste and surface of meat, these developments vow to lessen the ecological impression of meat creation while fulfilling the developing interest for protein-rich food varieties.

Food innovation is additionally reshaping the way that we access and eat food, with the ascent of food conveyance applications, dinner unit administrations, and online staple stages making it simpler than any time in recent memory to appreciate café quality feasts in the solace of our homes. In the interim, brilliant kitchen machines outfitted with computerized reasoning and web availability are smoothing out the cooking system, giving customized recipe suggestions, and limiting food squander by streamlining fixing utilization and capacity.

Yet, as we embrace these mechanical progressions, taking into account their likely advantages and challenges is fundamental. While lab-developed meat and plant-based options offer a promising answer for the ecological effect of creature horticulture, they likewise bring up issues about security, administrative oversight, and shopper acknowledgment. Likewise, while food conveyance applications and brilliant kitchen machines offer accommodation and proficiency, they additionally raise worries about work rehearses, information protection, and the disintegration of conventional culinary abilities and information.

As we explore the crossing point of innovation and food development, let us approach these progressions with interest, decisive reasoning, and a pledge to guaranteeing that they serve everyone's benefit. By bridling the force of innovation to make a more manageable, fair, and flavorful food framework, we can prepare for a more promising time to come for food and humankind the same.

Social Variety and Culinary Trade:

Set out on a culinary excursion that commends the rich embroidery of worldwide cooking, where social variety and culinary trade join to make an energetic and dynamic food scene. In this part, we investigate the significant meaning of social variety in forming the eventual fate of food, featuring the significance of multifaceted figuring out, culinary the travel industry, and the safeguarding of culinary legacy.

Social variety is at the core of our worldwide food experience, with each dish recounting an account of history, custom, and character. From the zesty curries of India to the tart ceviches of Peru, the world's culinary practices are basically as different as the way of life that produce them, mirroring the novel flavors, fixings, and cooking methods of every locale.

Be that as it may, social variety isn't just about the food — it's likewise about individuals behind the dishes, the narratives they tell, and the customs they maintain. Culinary the travel industry offers a window into the spirit of a culture, giving a potential chance to investigate new flavors, find out about various culinary practices, and associate with neighborhood networks in significant and legitimate ways.

In an undeniably interconnected world, culinary trade fills in as an amazing asset for cultivating diverse comprehension and advancing harmony and congruity among countries. By sharing feasts, trading recipes, and embracing the flavors and elements of various societies, we can connect separates, challenge generalizations, and assemble associations that rise above lines and limits.

In any case, as we commend the variety of worldwide cooking, it's fundamental to perceive the significance of safeguarding culinary legacy and guaranteeing that conventional culinary practices and information are passed down to people in the future. By respecting the culinary customs of our predecessors and supporting native foodways, we can safeguard social variety and advance food power, guaranteeing that each local area has the privilege to feed itself in manners that are socially, socially, and earth maintainable.

As we plan ahead for food, let us embrace the lavishness and variety of worldwide cooking, commending the flavors, customs, and stories that make our reality so delightfully different. By embracing social variety and culinary trade, we can make a future where food isn't simply food yet a festival of our common mankind. Bon appétit, and may your culinary experiences be as different and improving as the actual world.

Food Squander Decrease and Round Economy:

Enter an existence where waste turns into a remnant of the past, as we investigate procedures and drives pointed toward diminishing food squander and progressing to a roundabout food economy. In this part, we dive into the natural, social, and monetary advantages of limiting food squander, from fertilizing the soil and food recuperation projects to reasonable bundling and store network enhancement.

Food squander is a squeezing worldwide issue, with roughly 33% of all food delivered for human utilization being lost or squandered every year. Besides the fact that this waste addresses a huge wasting of assets, yet it likewise adds to ecological corruption, ozone depleting substance emanations, and food weakness. By tending to food squander, we can ease yearning and destitution as well as moderate the effect of food creation on environmental change and biodiversity misfortune.

One of the best ways of decreasing food squander is through fertilizing the soil, where food scraps and natural waste are changed into supplement rich soil alterations for use in nurseries and horticulture. Fertilizing the soil redirects natural waste from landfills as well as assists with renewing soil wellbeing and richness, shutting the circle on the food creation cycle and advancing a more feasible and regenerative way to deal with horticulture.

Food recuperation programs offer one more answer for food squander, diverting excess food from ranches, cafés, and supermarkets to those out of luck. By reallocating consumable however unsold food to food banks, asylums, and local area associations, these projects help to mitigate hunger and lessen food squander while advancing social value and supporting neighborhood networks.

Maintainable bundling is likewise a basic part of lessening food squander, as it assists with broadening the time span of usability of transitory food sources and limit the ecological effect of bundling materials. From compostable bundling produced using plant-based materials to reusable compartments and imaginative bundling arrangements intended to limit food decay, reasonable bundling offers a pathway to a more round and without waste food framework.

As we investigate the eventual fate of food squander decrease and the roundabout economy, let us embrace the standards of lessen, reuse, and reuse in our regular routines, limiting waste at every possible opportunity and supporting drives that advance a more economical and evenhanded food framework for all. By co-operating to handle food squander, we can make a future where each dinner is a festival of overflow, feeding the two individuals and the planet.

Customized Nourishment and Wellbeing:

Set out on an excursion into the domain of customized nourishment and health, where state of the art innovations and logical headways unite to fit dietary proposals and wellbeing plans to individual necessities and inclinations. In this part, we investigate the arising patterns in customized sustenance, from DNA-based diets and wearable wellbeing trackers to customized dinner conveyance benefits, and look at their expected effect on wellbeing results, dietary propensities, and the fate of food utilization.

Customized nourishment is a change in outlook by they way we approach diet and wellbeing, creating some distance from one-size-fits-every dietary proposal and towards a more individualized and all encompassing way to deal with wellbeing. By utilizing hereditary data, biomarkers, and way of life information, custom-ized sustenance tries to distinguish the exceptional wholesome necessities and metabolic profiles of every person, taking into con-sideration designated dietary intercessions that improve wellbeing and prosperity.

Perhaps of the most encouraging advancement in customized nourishment is the approach of DNA-based consumes less calories, which utilize hereditary testing to distinguish hereditary varia-tions related with supplement digestion, food bigotries, and illness risk. By examining a person's hereditary profile, DNA-based diets can give customized dietary suggestions custom-made to their novel hereditary cosmetics, assisting with enhancing supplement admission, forestall persistent sickness, and further develop generally speaking wellbeing results.

Wearable wellbeing trackers offer one more road for customized nourishment, giving constant information on active work, rest examples, and dietary propensities to assist people with settling on informed conclusions about their wellbeing and health. By following key measurements like calorie admission, macronutrient equilibrium, and hydration levels, wearable wellbeing trackers can enable people to assume command over their wellbeing and make positive way of life changes.

Customized dinner conveyance administrations address a further development in customized sustenance, offering redid feast plans and recipes custom-made to individual dietary inclinations, wellbeing objectives, and culinary inclinations. By removing the mystery from dinner arranging and readiness, these administrations make it more straightforward than at any other time for people to follow customized dietary proposals and keep up with smart dieting propensities.

As we embrace the capability of customized nourishment and health, perceiving the significance of a reasonable and comprehensive way to deal with health is fundamental. While customized nourishment can give significant experiences into individual dietary requirements and inclinations, it's urgent to consider different factors like social, ecological, and social impacts on wellbeing and prosperity. By consolidating customized nourishment with an all encompassing way to deal with health, we can make a future where each individual has the instruments and information they need to accomplish ideal wellbeing and essentialness.

{ **8** }

Chapter 8: Conclusion

Recap of Key Subjects:

As we reach the finish of our culinary excursion, it's fundamental to consider the vital subjects and experiences that have molded our investigation of worldwide cooking. All through this book, we have dove into the rich embroidery of culinary customs from around the world, uncovering the different flavors, fixings, and procedures that make each culture's food extraordinary.

From the hot curries of India to the sensitive sushi of Japan, we have praised the excellence of social variety and culinary trade, perceiving the significant effect of history, geology, and custom on the food varieties we love. We have discovered that food isn't simply food however a strong articulation of personality, local area, and shared humankind, rising above lines and limits to join us in a common appreciation for the delights of the table.

In any case, our investigation of worldwide cooking has likewise uncovered the difficulties and potential open doors confronting our food frameworks in the 21st 100 years. We have faced issues of supportability, food uncertainty, and social allotment, wrestling with the complicated real factors of a globalized food scene. However, in the midst of these difficulties, we have found the capability of food development, innovation, and aggregate activity to make a more evenhanded, strong, and delectable future for food.

As we recap the key subjects investigated in this book — culinary variety, social trade, supportability, and advancement — we are helped to remember the force of food to feed both body and soul, to associate us to our foundations and to one another. Whether we're imparting a feast to friends and family, investigating new flavors in our own kitchens, or supporting for an all the more and maintainable food framework, let us convey forward the examples gained from our culinary excursion and keep on commending the kinds of the world with happiness, interest, and appreciation.

Reflection on Culinary Excursion:

As we delay to consider the culinary excursion we've set out upon together, let us appreciate the recollections of the flavors investigated, the dishes relished, and the tales shared. All through this book, we've navigated landmasses and crossed seas, drenching ourselves in the rich embroidery of worldwide cooking and finding the significant associations between food, culture, and personality.

Our culinary excursion has been something other than a mission for heavenly dinners — it has been a journey of revelation, a festival of variety, and a demonstration of the force of food to unite individuals. We've tasted the searing flavors of the Center East, the fragrant spices of Southeast Asia, and the generous solace food sources of Europe, each dish recounting an account of history, custom, and development.

Be that as it may, our process has additionally been one of learning and development, as we've wrestled with complex issues like supportability, food equity, and social appointment. We've stood up to the unforgiving real factors of our worldwide food framework — the stunning degrees of food squander, the imbalances of food access, and the ecological effect of modern horticulture — and we've been tested to imagine an all the more and feasible future for food.

However, in the midst of the difficulties, our culinary excursion has been imbued with trust and motivation, as we've experienced the strength of limited scope ranchers, the resourcefulness of cooks, and the enthusiasm of food activists attempting to make positive change in their networks. We've perceived how food has the ability to sustain our bodies as well as our spirits, cultivating associations, encouraging comprehension, and cultivating euphoria in the straightforward demonstration of imparting a dinner to friends and family.

As we consider the culinary excursion we've shared, let us convey forward the illustrations learned and the recollections made, esteeming the extravagance of our worldwide food legacy and conceding to building a more reasonable, fair, and delectable future for food. Whether we're cooking a customary family recipe, supporting neighborhood ranchers, or pushing for food equity, let us keep on commending the kinds of the world with appreciation, modesty, and love for the inconceivable endowment of food.

Source of inspiration:

As we close our investigation of worldwide food, now is the right time to interpret our freshly discovered information and appreciation right into it. Every one of us plays a part to play in forming the fate of food, and right now is an ideal opportunity to subscribe to having a constructive outcome in our own lives and networks.

Above all else, let us focus on growing our culinary skylines by investigating new flavors, foods, and fixings from around the world. Whether it's difficult another recipe at home, visiting a nearby ethnic market, or feasting at a local eatery serving credible worldwide cooking, let us embrace the variety of worldwide food culture and praise the extravagance of our common culinary legacy.

Second, let us focus on manageability in our food decisions, supporting practices that limit ecological effect, moderate regular assets, and advance biodiversity. This might include picking privately obtained and occasional fixings, decreasing food squander through careful feast arranging and fertilizing the soil, or supporting ranchers and makers who focus on manageable and regenerative farming practices.

Third, let us advocate for food equity and value, attempting to guarantee that everybody approaches nutritious, reasonable, and socially significant food. This might include supporting strategies and drives that address food weakness, pushing for fair wages and working circumstances for food laborers, or chipping in with associations that work to lighten yearning and destitution in our networks.

Fourth, let us embrace development and imagination in our way to deal with food, investigating new advances, culinary strategies, and food drifts that can possibly reform the manner in which we eat and associate with food. Whether it's exploring different avenues regarding plant-based cooking, supporting food new companies that are creating economical options in contrast to conventional creature items, or putting resources into kitchen devices that smooth out feast planning and decrease food squander, let us embrace the soul of advancement and trial and error in our culinary experiences.

At last, let us focus on encouraging associations and building local area through food, perceiving that the demonstration of sharing a feast has the ability to separate boundaries, span partitions, and manufacture significant connections. Whether it's facilitating a potluck supper with companions and neighbors, sorting out a local area cooking class, or chipping in at a nearby food bank, let us use food as an impetus for association, discussion, and cooperation.

As we leave on this excursion of culinary investigation and move, let us recall that each chomp we initiate, every feast we share, and every decision we make has the ability to shape the fate of nourishment for a long time into the future. Together, let us make an existence where food isn't simply food yet a wellspring of delight, association, and opportunities for all.

Vision for What's to come:

As we plan ahead for food, let us imagine an existence where culinary variety is praised, food frameworks are manageable and evenhanded, and each individual approaches nutritious and socially pertinent dinners. In this vision, food isn't simply an item however a wellspring of sustenance, delight, and association — an impression of our common humankind and our obligation to building a superior world for all.

In this future, our worldwide food framework is portrayed by strength, variety, and overflow, with limited scope ranchers and food makers assuming a focal part in taking care of their networks and managing the land. Food is developed, gathered, and appropriated in manners that regard the world's normal assets, limit squander, and advance biodiversity, guaranteeing that people in the future can keep on partaking in the abundance of our planet into the indefinite future.

In this future, food is likewise a wellspring of civil rights and value, with everybody approaching nutritious and socially suitable feasts no matter what their pay, race, or foundation. Food weakness is a relic of days gone by, as networks meet up to help each other, share assets, and supporter for strategies that guarantee that nobody goes hungry in a universe of bounty.

In this future, culinary practices are safeguarded and celebrated, with each culture's special food legacy esteemed and regarded. Food turns into an extension that interfaces us to our underlying foundations, our predecessors, and one another, encouraging grasping, sympathy, and appreciation for the wealth of our common human experience.

In this future, advancement and imagination flourish, with gourmet specialists, food business people, and researchers cooperating to foster better approaches for delivering, planning, and getting a charge out of food that are both delectable and supportable. From lab-developed meat and plant-based options in contrast to vertical cultivating and 3D-printed food, the potential outcomes are huge, offering energizing open doors to rethink the manner in which we eat and connect with food.

As we make progress toward this vision for the eventual fate of food, let us recollect that change begins with every last one of us. Whether it's deciding to help neighborhood ranchers, lessening food squander in our own homes, or pushing for strategies that advance food equity and supportability, let us each do our part to make a future where food isn't simply a method for endurance yet a wellspring of bliss, association, and overflow for all.

Closing Considerations:

As we arrive at the finish of our culinary excursion, let us delay to think about the examples took in, the flavors relished, and the associations fashioned en route. Our investigation of worldwide cooking has been a demonstration of the influence of food to feed body and soul, to interface us to our underlying foundations and to one another, and to rouse us to embrace the wealth and variety of our reality.

As we bid goodbye to the pages of this book, let us convey forward the soul of interest, transparency, and appreciation that has directed our excursion. Allow us to keep on investigating new flavors, search out new culinary encounters, and commend the way of life and customs that make our reality so delightfully different.

In any case, let us additionally recollect that our process doesn't end here. The universe of food is immense and always showing signs of change, with new fixings to find, new recipes to attempt, and new stories to share. Whether we're preparing a family feast, imparting a potluck to companions, or eating at an eatery serving cooking from across the globe, let us approach each culinary experience with satisfaction, interest, and worship for the staggering endowment of food.

As we close the book on this section of our culinary excursion, let us express appreciation for the sustenance it has given, the experiences it has offered, and the associations it has encouraged. What's more, let us anticipate the numerous culinary experiences that lie ahead, realizing that every dinner we share, each dish we taste, and each chomp we appreciate is a valuable chance to praise the magnificence and overflow of our reality. Bon appétit, and may your culinary undertakings be basically as rich and remunerating as the kinds of worldwide food.